Born *for* Heaven

Playing with Angels

Phyllis Beltz

BORN FOR
Heaven

Playing with Angels

Phyllis Beltz

Inspiring Voices®
A Service of **Guideposts**

Scripture quotations taken from the New American Standard Bible®, Copyright © 1960, 1962, 1963, 1968, 1971, 1972, 1973, 1975, 1977, 1995 by The Lockman Foundation. Used by permission. (www.Lockman.org)

Inspiring Voices books may be ordered through booksellers or by contacting:

Inspiring Voices
1663 Liberty Drive
Bloomington, IN 47403
www.inspiringvoices.com
1-(866) 697-5313

ISBN: 978-1-4624-0283-0 (sc)
ISBN: 978-1-4624-0284-7 (e)

Library of Congress Control Number: 2012914928

Printed in the United States of America

Inspiring Voices rev. date: 08/16/2012

To Jake, Christopher's best friend

Contents

Preface

Thank you for joining me in this journey into the kind of deep sorrow that engulfs your entire being when faced with the death of your child. This is a journey I did not want to take and one that I believed had passed me by since my children were grown. Then those little heart stealers known as grandchildren entered into my life. This is where the story begins as my husband and I became parents again when we took two grandchildren into our home and hearts to rear Then the unthinkable happened, my ten year old grandchild was dead, killed by a school bus.

You will journey with me into and through to the other side of my dark valley of despair. I felt as if I had been thrown into a pit with a force harsh enough to destroy me. I was not alone for Jesus was with me every step of the way and brought me safely through the darkness into His marvelous light.

When we encounter any kind of tragedy in our life whether it is a death, illness, financial, or any other disruption in our normal everyday living we need to ask; "What did I learn?"

First let me say I am still learning from this incident in my life. I don't suppose I will ever stop learning and that is a good thing. I have much to learn and reflect on my life and my interaction with others going through tough times. I believe the most important thing I learned is never miss the chance to say "I love you." Never miss the chance to give someone a hug, just because!

I have learned that no child fits into another's mold and must be cared for and taught in the way that best benefits that child. Not every child is a straight A student or a rock star but a precious individual who can learn and understand about Jesus and how much He loves them. You can teach them they are number one with Jesus and He will always be cheering them on even if the world doesn't

In writing this book my desire is that it gives comfort and hope to anyone who has lost a child. There is hope and help in the Scripture. I want this story to challenge you in at least two ways. One is that you would get serious about making in-depth study of God's Word a part of your life so you are prepared to handle the unexpected. The benefit will not only be yours but you then will be able to be a comfort and encourager to others when tragedy strikes. Another is to start teaching your children at a young age about Jesus and if they are older it is never too late to start.

My prayer is that God will be glorified in the telling of Christopher's story.

1

A Parent's Worst Fear

Friday February 6, 2009, my Dad's birthday, the streets were still ice and snow covered from the recent snow storms. I took my grandson Christopher to his home school and from there he took a school bus to another school where he attended special needs classes.

One hour and a half later three people stood on my front porch and the man with the badge introduced himself as an official from the police department. I recognized the other man as Christopher's teacher and the other person was the woman in charge of placing Christopher in this special class. They said they needed to come in. I ask if something was wrong with Christopher. Three times they said "we need to come in," Panic began to well up inside me and never could I have been prepared for what I was about to hear. When they got inside I said "What's wrong is something wrong with Christopher?" They said "We need to go into the other room." When they got me near a chair the policeman said "Christopher has been killed by a school bus." No softening of the message, just a harsh statement. I nearly collapsed and he got me safely to a chair. I cried "Oh no dear God, not my baby, not my Christopher." His next statement sent an abnormal chill through my body and much of what happened immediately after this is hard to remember. I was numb! It seemed as if my mind and body were shutting down. He informed me that Christopher had not been taken to the hospital but straight to the morgue. This was the final blow. I couldn't believe what I was hearing; I couldn't process what he had said. This can't be happening. This isn't real. I didn't even ask what had happened. I sat and sobbed. When they were ready to leave I ask "How could this have happened that a school bus killed him?" No one answered me; I believe they were in shock also. The details had been given to my son and I didn't want to hear them.

Next I called the church for the prayer line and within minutes every pastor in the church called to offer prayers and comfort all in disbelief at what had happened. I called a student in my Precept Bible class, then a neighbor. My son finished the calls after the police gave him the details. By this time the accident was being reported every hour on the hour on every radio and television program. Later I was told the news went state wide and even later was told many churches in Indiana had prayer for us in their weekend services. The news coverage went on for days but I did not listen or watch TV afraid they might give too many details that I could not handle.

As soon as his name was released by the media it wasn't long before people started streaming into the house and the phone never stopped ringing. One neighbor whose children were playmates of Christopher was at the pharmacy when she heard his name announced on the television. She left immediately saying "I've got to go, I will come back, that's our Christopher." She was one of many that rushed to be with me when they heard the news.

Everyone was stunned by the news and there seemed to be no words to convey their feelings so they just cried with me. As the day went on people brought food and flowers and several friends stayed all day with me. Several times through the tears someone would share something about Christopher that would bring a smile to our tear stained faces. This was a comfort and blessing I will never forget. Every person offered spiritual comfort and in the coming weeks many assured me that Christopher's angel snatched him up so quickly and gave him to Jesus so fast that he did not suffer.

Even though I wasn't at the scene of the accident I could picture in my mind what happened. The picture of the bus hitting him and running over him is imbedded in my mind and it intrudes unwanted like a bolt of lightning with the same jolting effect as if I had been hit by the bus myself. This comes at unexpected and unusual times and causes me much agony and sadness. I have been abruptly awakened at night with the scene playing in my mind. When I see a school bus on TV or when I am driving in the car and see one the tears start flowing.

Two days before the accident I had made the decision to take Christopher out of this special program. I thought it best to wait until the semester was over and I needed the time to decide what I was going to do with him. There were many choices but in the time since the accident I have thought many times that I hoped my choice would have been home schooling. I have imagined how I could use his love of cooking to help him to exercise his creative bent and teach him about fractions and spelling just from the cooking lessons. I have wondered many times since the accident why I didn't act sooner and I even feel guilty about not doing so. I also know that I can't go there; I can't dwell on "if only."

2

The Beginning

There are many stories to tell about our lives in the ten years my husband and I raised our two grandchildren yet that is not the purpose of this story. I will set the stage with only the highlights. We were so unhappy and embarrassed when we learned our daughter was pregnant and unmarried. That all changed the minute we saw our grandson. He became ours in our hearts from that moment on as did his sister when she was born under the same circumstances in 2002. My husband died in 2006 but when he knew the time was getting close his main concern was about the grandchildren and how they would handle his death.

Christopher was six weeks old when we made the first rescue of his mother and him. We only had a days' notice to get ready for them before the out of state trip to bring them back to our home. We spent that day getting a crib and putting it together and buying all we would need for a new baby. This was our first look at our grandchild and we fell in love with him. After the long trip home my husband monopolized Christopher rocking him talking to him until I finally said "Do I get to hold him too?" This little guy had won our hearts.

Eighteen days later we left the house for the evening to attend our son's oldest boys' basketball game. This is our first grandson who shares Christmas birthday with Christopher. What fun to have two grandchildren with Christmas birthdays! It was hard to leave the baby that evening and I went back into the baby's room twice to kiss him goodbye. Little did I know those would be the last kisses for some time. We came home to an eerily quiet house and we knew even before we noticed the note left for us by his mother that they were gone along with most of the baby items we had purchased. We were devastated for we had no idea where they had gone. This would be just the beginning of the tears we would shed and the problems we would encounter as we tried to keep this baby safe.

We did not hear from her for five months. It was now summer and she called to let us know she was still in town. Every week from then on she would get someone to bring her and Christopher to visit us. It wasn't long before she started leaving Christopher with us for days at a time.

When he was eleven months old we had another dramatic rescue of both of them. After this rescue Christopher and his mother lived with us thirteen months. Christopher was now two years old. I was out of town attending a Bible Conference and my husband was at work when he called and said "They're gone again." The next and last time we rescued them was when Christopher was three and half years old. This time there was a new addition, five month old Hannah. Their mother stayed with us for ten months and then left saying that she knew she could not raise the children and we would do a better job. We found an apartment for her near us so she could be close enough that she could visit us often. We now had permanent custody of the children

We lived in a condo for several years but now my husband decided we should have a house with a yard for the children so he had a house built for us. One year and ten months after moving into our new home my husband died. It was now just the three of us. This was very hard on the children and they missed their Papa so much. In retrospect I am glad my husband was not alive when Christopher was killed because I believe he would have not recovered from the heartbreak of this terrible tragedy. He was so in love with both of those children. Four months after the accident the business my husband started forty years before was one of the auto dealerships that was closed by Chrysler and then when they declared bankruptcy there was no compensation for my son who was now the primary owner and for me as part owner. It seemed as if bad things were not going to stop.

The focus of this book is not on these events but about Christopher and his love of life, his love for Jesus and the church. It is also a story about a compassionate God Who never left my side during this traumatic time. In the night when I couldn't sleep I felt the quiet tender love of Jesus saying through His memorized Word "I am here, I will not leave you or forsake you. Rest in Me." How I thank Precept Ministries Inductive Study for teaching me through the years how to study God's Word and how to know God in a way I never had before along with the memorization of Scripture. I had been a Precept Workshop Trainer for the Ministry for several years until the grandchildren came to live with us permanently. It was now time to put into practice lessons I had learned and taught to others.

One of those nights of not sleeping I was in such distress and said to the Lord, "All we wanted to do was to keep those children safe and get them back home to You." He gently said, "You did and he is. He is home with Me." So many times right after the accident I was in such distress I could not stay out of bed long enough to accomplish any task. On one of those rare occasions when I did get up and try to do something constructive I told a friend, "Every time I turn to do something I bump right into Jesus. It is like He is glued to me and won't let me stay in this dark pit of despair by myself."

3

Christopher and Jesus

*C*hristopher loved to go to church and he loved to hear about Jesus. He had a smile that came right from his heart to his eyes and his eyes would light up when he talked about Jesus. Studio 6 - 7 is the name for the children's wing taken from Deuteronomy 6:7 "And you shall teach them diligently to your sons and shall talk of them when you sit in your house and when you walk by the way and when you lie down and when you rise up." His destination each week upon leaving the Studio was to head for the big room (his name for the sanctuary) and stand on the stage and pretend he was either singing or talking about Jesus. One time he started crying very loudly and I couldn't get him quiet and the Pastor came quickly to my rescue asking what was wrong and could he help? I said "He doesn't want to go home" He laughed and said that was what he liked to hear.

Hannah who is ten now and Christopher both were open to talking about heaven, Jesus and death. They were very attached to my husband and his death was hard on them. He was the only father they knew and my husband was crazy about both of them and spent a lot of time with them. When my husband died Christopher was eight years old and Hannah four years so at that age they had many questions about heaven and death.

I told them both about how wonderful Jesus is and how much he loves them. We watched various videos for children about Jesus, His life and crucifixion. The Veggie Tales videos were watched almost daily. They especially liked to play with the game of Resurrection Eggs and open each one to find the symbol of the crucifixion. They would take turns opening an egg and tell what the symbol was and the story about that symbol. Children respond very well to items they can talk about and hold in their hands. One year we baked Easter Story Cookies which is a two day project but well worth the time when on Easter morning they take a bite of a cookie that has been in the oven over night and are amazed to find it is hollow; to find it empty inside. On the first Easter Jesus' followers were amazed to find the tomb open and empty. You can find this recipe on the internet under Resurrection Cookie Recipe. At Christmas time they had their own unbreakable nativity set that intrigued them especially the glowing angel. Every now and then the baby Jesus would disappear but was found clutched in one of their hands or stashed in their room. Reading was always an important activity for both of them and in their library they had many Christian books. As a parent or grandparent I would urge you to surround the children in the home with these type of activities. They are never too young to grasp the story of Jesus.

Almost every night we would gather in the family room and the two of them would dance and sing to a CD of children's praise music. Christopher would serenade us by playing his guitar. One time when I was lying on the couch ill, he stood beside me and played his guitar and sang to me to make me feel better. This was a real incentive to get well because he really hadn't grasped the know-how of the guitar! Mainly we talked a lot about Jesus and heaven. After their dancing and singing we would quiet down by reading books. When reading books we always read the Title, Author and Illustrator so they could get the full effect of reading the entire book. This session would end with each one of us making up a silly story. Children love to laugh and they need some times of silliness. When Hannah learned to print she began writing her stories in a notebook and later she added drawings to her stories. Then she decided that someday she might like to be an author and if she does I hope she remembers where and when the love of reading was introduced to her. A few times I would say "O.K. kids how about we have a party tonight." They both would say in unison "Can Jesus come?" They worked together to set a place for Him at the table, always making sure they had the right plates and silverware and never forgetting the napkin. What a fun way to learn how to set a table! Their conversation sounded just as if Jesus was present in the flesh at our party.

I taught them about the Rapture of the Church as it is explained in I Thessalonians 4:14-17 "For if we believe that Jesus died and rose again, even so God will bring with Him those who have fallen asleep in Jesus. For this we say to you by the word of the Lord, that we who are alive and remain until the coming of the Lord, will not precede those who have fallen asleep. For the Lord Himself will descend from heaven with a shout, with the voice of the archangel and the trumpet of God, and the dead in Christ will rise first. Then we who are alive and remain will be caught up together with them in the clouds to meet the Lord in the air, and so we shall always be with the Lord." Just the other day Hannah said to me "What was that you told Christopher and me about Jesus coming in the sky on a cloud and we would go up in the air?" So even at her young age she remembers our conversations about Jesus

Grandparents reading this will remember a less hectic time in their childhood when looking for pictures in the clouds could occupy a great deal of play time. The goal was to hope the illusive cloud picture we saw would keep its shape until our fellow cloud watcher could see the same picture we were sure we saw. What a delight for me to introduce this past time to my grandchildren. One time when we were in the car Christopher very excitedly and loudly said "Oh look up in the clouds, that looks like Jesus, JESUS IS COMING." Hannah said "Show me I want to see Him too." It seemed that Christopher had Jesus on his mind very often.

Another time Christopher wanted to hear the Rapture story again and when I finished telling him what would happen at that time he ask "Will you hold my hand when we go up in the air?" I said "I sure will" and he grabbed and hugged me and his eyes sparkled with delight. Then he ask me "Mama when I go to heaven will I be able to have my toys with me?" I replied "Oh honey if you want your toys I am sure they will be there but do you know what is going to be even better? Any time you want a hug Jesus is going to be right there beside you and give you the biggest hug you have ever had." He jumped up from his chair and his eyes were dancing sparkling bright and he said "REALLY, it sounds so wonderful I want to go right now." It wasn't long after this he went to heaven. That is my fondest memory of our conversations about Jesus and heaven.

~⊙ 4 ⊙~

Best Friends

*C*hristopher met his best friend Jake when Jake's mother Kristine Barnett started Jacob's Place. This is a sports program for autism which included all children with various problems not just autism. Jake has a mild form of autism called aspersers and is the same age as Christopher. Jake is also a genius with a very high IQ and has taken college courses since he was ten years old. Christopher did not have autism but had a thought process disorder with autistic tendencies.

The program was held at my church but not connected with the church. This was good for Christopher because he felt safe being at the church property. Jake and Christopher spent hours on the phone and played basketball and worked on magic tricks together. They visited back and forth at each home playing with their cars and trucks. They ate together, went swimming together with Jakes two younger brothers.

The night of the accident the entire Barnett family came to the house and stayed for a long time. What a comfort and blessing that was for me. I have come to appreciate the time people have given to me during this tragic time and I am convicted of times I failed to respond and minister to someone dealing with a tragedy. Jake sat on the couch cradling some of Christopher's toys sobbing so hard he could not talk. As they were leaving I ask him if he would like to take the toys he had in his hands. He said through his sobs that he would like that very much. The two younger boys also were given toys of Christopher's.

Private services were held on Monday and friends and family were invited to my house for lunch and as Hannah said "a celebration". Jake and his mother came to the house and this time Jake sat on the couch head down curled in his mother's arms refusing to talk. I went to him twice but no response from him. Finally his Mom said he spoke to her and told her he did not like the smiles on people's faces and the laughter. He said "They should look like I feel on the inside and I hurt." She decided it was best for them to leave because he was getting more and more upset. When they arrived home Kristine called to tell me that on the way home Jake said "I didn't think angels were supposed to be jealous but I think they watched Christopher playing and having so much fun they decided it was their turn to play with him." There is an even more exciting story concerning Jake and his family which I deal with later.

✒❀5❀✒

Goodbye

We thought only a few people would come to the house after the funeral but we were wrong. Friends stood outside in the icy cold weather an hour to even get into the house. My son and his wife have a wonderful group of friends who took over the food service and had planned for a large crowd bringing so much equipment and food that my house looked like a smorgasbord restaurant. What a blessing to have people take over chores that you are unable to attend to during this stressful time.

Christopher was well known in the neighborhood for loving to ride his bike and he was especially proud of his new red bike he got for Christmas which is also his birthday. On Saturday the day after the accident the neighborhood children had their own unique way of saying goodbye to Christopher. They worked together with help from their parents and put Christopher's bike on the front porch and began to decorate the shiny red bike he loved so much. Each one brought a variety of memories of their neighborhood playmate. They brought drawings, poems, toys, and pictures and put them in a basket they tied to the bike. They made a large poster with pictures of Christopher and notes of what they remembered and loved about him. There was a mini basketball, deck of cards for his tricks, magic wand, and small cars. The girls wrote "Who wasn't Christopher's girlfriend?" He liked the girls! One mother tied some sticks together with miniature marshmallows and wrote a note that said; on the coldest day in the winter Christopher knocked on my door and inquired; "Is this a good day for a bond fire and marshmallows?" Her answer to him was of course they would have one in a day or so when she could get it all together. She was true to her word and on a very cold winter day the neighborhood kids had a marshmallow roast and pizza and fun.

I left the bicycle on the porch day and night and the children would come one or two or three at a time and stand quietly and look at the memorabilia. Sometimes they would talk to one another and sometimes they would ring the doorbell and when I opened the door they stepped in and just stood looking at me not saying a word. I would hug them and they would leave as they struggled to keep the tears from flowing. The neighbors were wonderful in showing their concern for me and brought food to me for three months. This was great because I had no energy or incentive to cook. One family from the neighborhood came to the house several times over the next few months and each time the father cried so hard saying how he loved Christopher and how very sorry he was about the accident. Christopher had made an impact on the entire neighborhood.

Christopher and I normally attended Saturday evening Church, but after the accident I could no longer handle the night time drive alone so I changed to Sunday service. I spent many Saturday evenings listening to the Gaither's Gospel music program and crying my eyes out wondering how I could have so many tears left in me. Truly Saturday night became the loneliest night of the week. One Saturday night about two months after the funeral two boys from the neighborhood rang my door bell and said they wanted to come tell me how much they loved and miss Christopher and could they look at all the memorabilia again? It was still set up in the back hall. They enjoyed looking at the items and quietly talking about all he loved and pointing out their pictures and poems. One of the mothers had made a picture album of Christopher from pictures she had taken when all the kids in the neighborhood had been at her house for parties. It brought back good memories for the boys. When they left each one gave me a hug. I had been crying before they came and now I was really crying but I felt as if I had received a hug from Jesus.

Thanks for the Memories

BIKES

Three months after the accident two mothers in the neighborhood contacted Freewheelin' Bike Organization, a bike safety program, to set up a day in honor of Christopher. It was held at Christopher's home school and over seventy bikes were collected that day. Not only do they give bicycle safety tips but the donated bikes put several people to work repairing the bikes which are then donated or sold. Jake attended this event but it was too much for him and we had to take him inside the school for a while to get him away from the noise and the crowd and the emotion of this event for Christopher.

SCHOOL GARDEN

I understand Jakes emotional response to anything concerning Christopher because I too am overcome with emotion when it comes to the memory of Christopher. One day my mailbox was bulging with a large package that had a return address of his school.

What I found in that box was enough emotion to make me want to respond as Jake did and get away from it all. The first item I found was Christopher's extra clothing kept at the school for emergencies. I broke down and cried. When I got over the shock of seeing his clothes that he would never wear again I dug into the large box and there I found a notebook full of a treasure of condolences from his school mates, teachers and parents. The children in the lower grades contributed crayon drawings of flowers and hearts and scrawled messages. The higher grades wrote notes about how sorry they were about the accident. They offered their prayers and several said they hoped we would all feel better soon. There were cards and notes from the teachers and parents that spoke of his sparking eyes and love of life. By the time I read the last note I was emotionally drained. From the things the children shared in their pictures and writing I knew it had to be difficult for each one to get their thoughts on paper. I could sense the emotion in the notes from the parents and I am sure many were written with tears in their eyes. It was a sobering time that touched all their lives and I am sure the memory of the raw emotions they felt will fade in time but the incident will never be forgotten.

Enclosed also was a note telling me that two people had contributed several hundred dollars toward a memorial garden for Christopher to be in the atrium of the school. A large marker with his name has been placed beside a newly planted tree and surrounded by seasonal flowers which the PTA will maintain. I know this only through pictures that have been sent to me because I cannot bring myself to go anywhere near the school.

GRACE WORKS

My church has in the Children's Ministry a program called Grace Works. This takes place in the weekend services and is for children with any kind of special needs. In order to serve these special children the parents give written information concerning specifics about the kind of care their child might need. It helps to know if there is something that might frighten the child or signs of a meltdown. Information is needed to know what can be done to soothe and comfort the child. Sometimes it's a hug that reassures them, maybe a walk outside, something to eat or a soothing drink. Shooting baskets is always an option. A volunteer Grace Giver is assigned to each child. This will be the same person each week which is a comfort to the child with the result being this consistency brings about a special bond between Grace Giver and child.

Christopher's Grace Giver was a Dad and his son. The son was in Christopher's class but two years older. He had an interest in this type of service so he chose to be a part of Christopher's life at church. I felt so sorry for both of them when they came to the house the day of the funeral. They were crying so hard and the Dad said Christopher was like his own son.

The first year after the accident the church instituted the Christopher Beltz award in connection with the Grace Works program. The church serves a delicious dinner in appreciation for all the Grace Giver's and their families and a beautiful award is given to a special Grace Giver. This will be an annual award in memory of Christopher with a new recipient each year.

CLIMBING TREES

The year after the accident on Mother's day I received a Mother's day card from a neighbor. Enclosed were pictures of trees and a note. Here is a portion of the note.

As your friends and neighbors, we think of you often and hope you are doing well. This has been a long winter and a very wet spring. Fortunately the rain has provided a lush landscape for the summer. With summer comes children and this is what keeps Christopher in our hearts

Christopher often crosses our minds when we enter the neighborhood. We recollect his playing in the driveway and "directing traffic" from the safety of his front yard. His smile made us smile! You couldn't help recall your own childhood memories when you watched him play! He was a happy reminder of days gone by, especially when he learned to ride his bicycle. We discussed how we fondly remembered Christopher and wanted to memorialize him in a long and lasting way.

Last year we decided to plant ten trees on our property to represent his age. Seeing neighbor kids playing outside warms our hearts; thinking of Christopher warms our hearts as well. His ten short years of life will be remembered in this neighborhood as the trees grow and spread their branches toward heaven. God will know how much he is missed. Your beautiful grandson has touched so many hearts

The pictures show the trees planted around the grounds as if they are hugging the property which is a reminder of how much Christopher loved hugs! Six of these trees are "tree climbing trees" which brings memories of summer play time and reminded them of how much Christopher loved to play. One special tree is planted in a prominent place in their front yard. This tree has shiny leaves with attention getting large bright flowers. This they said reminded them of Christopher's vibrant personality.

All of these remembrances overwhelm me when I reflect about the thought and effort that has gone into each one given in memory of a little boy they had only known for a short time.

I will leave another memorial until later in the book but now I want to tell you how God used people to bless, encourage and comfort me during this time. Maybe some of these blessing that were so graciously given to me will give you an idea as to how you comfort others in a tragic situation.

~❧ 7 ❧~

Above and Beyond

*M*y heart is broken in pieces and I am devastated over this accident but each and every prayer, card, phone call, tears of others and kind words is a drop of love that is put in my heart to seal up the brokenness while here on earth awaiting for a complete healing when I will see and hold Christopher again in heaven. Until then every night I ask Jesus to give Christopher a hug for me.

Every Friday night my Life Group from church met in my home. Christopher loved this time and would stand outside and greet everyone directing and ushering them into the house. They always paid a lot of attention to him. He would have freedom while they were here to do what he wanted in the house which made him feel special and he would always join us to eat the snacks they so lavishly furnished each week When they left we both knew it was party time for us. We fixed ourselves more snacks they had left and snuggled together on the couch to watch TV and stay up as long as we could keep our eyes open.

The church has a service weekend once a year where all the Life Groups are given assignments around the city. There are no church services that weekend and we all wear T-shirts printed with the words The Church has left the building. One year my group and two others went to the inner city to sweep the streets. Someone brought small work gloves for Christopher. He loved the entire idea of participating with so many people in the fun atmosphere. He felt so important in those work gloves he worked doubly hard sweeping the streets with all the gusto he could muster. When our task was done the fun continued back at the church with a cook-out for all the happily tired and hungry workers.

The Sunday after the accident and before the funeral I didn't go to church. The Pastor announced in all the services about the accident. One woman in my Life Group came directly to my home after the service. She said "I thought if you don't want to see anyone that is O.K. but I am going anyway." I assured her I couldn't have been more pleased that she would be with me for a while since it was an absolutely awful day for me. She said "I knew you and Christopher had a special relationship when we were sitting in the car in the inner city and you playfully reached over and poked his tummy and he giggled and gave you the sweetest smile."

Soon after the accident another from my Life Group brought me a gift from the entire group. It was a bracelet with blue beads for Christopher's birth month, clear beads for mine and opals for my husbands. Between the beads were silver cubes, one row spelled PHYLLIS and one row spelled CHRISTOPHER. In the middle was a grandmothers heart and attached to that was an angel and a cross. It was made specifically in this manner so that when wearing it I would always feel as if Christopher were with me. The ear rings were angels and were given to my daughter.

I have been humbled by the thoughtful outpouring from people during this time. Each gift or card I received was given with a specific memory of Christopher which makes them even more special. Truly these friends have done above and beyond as they have grieved with me.

My husband was well liked at the cancer center where he received his treatments. He was always so kind to everyone. His favorite thing to do for the nurses was to keep them supplied with caramels from a local candy store. He delighted in learning which variety each liked so he could accommodate their taste buds. Sometimes the children and I would sit with him while he had his treatment and the nurses all knew the children and our story. When both my husband and Christopher died the owner of the candy store expressed his sorrow in an encouraging note wrapped around a huge box of caramels.

One of those nurses whom I had not heard from since my husband died sent me a figurine of a mother and child entitled "Childs' Touch" a little boy hugging his mother. Every time I gaze upon this thoughtful gift I remember Christopher's hugs for me and think about how excited he was to anticipate a hug from Jesus. I know without a doubt upon his entrance into heaven he received the best hug ever from Jesus.

Someone else brought me a figurine of an angel. I think of this as Christopher's angel. Many people brought me books, articles, poems, of comfort, devotionals and I devoured them like a hungry hunter anticipating the next meal of comfort I would receive. I read everything I could find about the death of a child and how other people handled the heartache of losing a child.

Hannah and Christopher attended a church in the neighborhood for pre-school and special summer classes. The women in the church made a knitted shawl for me with a note that said "Be comforted with God's love wrapped around you."

When I was at my lowest; the exact time when I needed encouragement is when the ringing of the phone would pierce the loneliness of that hour and pleasantly I was hearing words of comfort and encouragement that gave me strength. Cards and e-mails were devoured and cherished. These things are not by accident. This is our great God Who is touched by our infirmities and uses His people to bring comfort and encouragement to you at the precise hour you need a hug from Jesus.

This support and cheer came from people I saw often to people I hadn't seen for years. About a week after the funeral I received a package from a woman I used to work with at Women's Conferences in the Indianapolis area. I had not seen or heard from her for at least fifteen years. This woman had the complete care of her husband who had many serious health problems, Alzheimer's being one. As of this writing he has gone to be with the Lord. She is raising her son's two children and also helping her son who is still dealing with problems that brought about her raising his children. With all this responsibility and drain on her energy she still manages to conduct her weekly radio program on Christian radio. As I opened the package I could see peeking through the tissue paper a beautiful golden shawl but I was stunned by the note she enclosed.

"Phyllis, when you put this shawl around you, may you feel you are wrapped in God's love. I have asked the Lord that when you have a day that you feel as if you cannot go on any longer to give me your burden for that day."

Another drop of love! Thank you Lord. To know that people show they are hurting with you by various kinds of gifts and words is like a soothing balm to your emotions and spirit during the healing process of a tragedy. I am amazed at the creative sensitivity of these gifts and yet I shouldn't be because God uses

His people to do above and beyond what we expect. This is God being God through His people. "Now to Him who is able to do far more abundantly beyond all that we ask or think, according to the power that works within us." Ephesians 3:20

8

Basketball and Jesus

*C*hristopher loved playing basketball not as a team member but just shooting baskets any time of the day or night and in any weather. Snow and cold did not deter him from dribbling and shooting baskets at which he became very adept.

Kristine, Jakes mother, had an old building in a very small Indiana town that she planned to have remodeled to house Jacob's place. Her main goal was to build an indoor basketball court in honor of Christopher. When someone vandalized the building the town officials said she could no longer take her time with the remodeling but must do something about the building immediately. She did not have the funds needed to get the building in shape. Through a series of events she found there was a man from a Christian foundation who was refurbishing several buildings on the same street as her building and he agreed to purchase her building.

He had a building across the street from hers that would take less time and money to refurbish. He offered an idea about using this building instead of hers. As details were talked about it became apparent this was not going to be a long term investment. Kristine was looking for permanent housing for Jacobs Place but after refurbishing the lease would only be for two years. Kristine and her husband have such a burden for children dealing with not only the various areas of autism but also other childhood problems. This is a place for kids in Indiana who find it difficult to interact with other children due to either physical or emotional situations. They want it to be a safe, non-threatening place for those who need to feel like any other kid playing sports where they are loved and accepted. It needed to be permanent.

This man knew of her desire to have a basketball court inside the building. A date was set for Kristine and Jake to meet this man at her old building to see what could be done. As they were walking around and inspecting parts of the building and removing some debris they uncovered a complete basketball court! Jake was so upset that he took off running and they found him around the side of the building sitting and crying. By this time everyone had tears in their eyes. As a result of this, the man realized he had bought the building from her just one month after Christopher died and was so shaken that he was convinced God wanted him to give his all and not hold anything back. He said he would refurbish his building and leave the lease at ten years with the option to sign the property over to her at that time if the program is successful. He is going to put in a basketball court.

Kristine has a sister, who is a child prodigy, very much like Jacob. She is an artist and does many portraits of children. Kristine told her about uncovering the basketball court and she says she felt that God and Christopher were there in Jacob's Place and she wanted to show everyone. She wants to make a huge mural which will require hours and hours of work and time. She wants to paint Jesus and do mixed medium and make a very detailed and stunning painting, almost as detailed as stained glass, on a wall that is forty feet high right behind the basketball goal. Jesus will be surrounded by children and Christopher will be painted at the feet of Jesus looking into his eyes. What a beautiful memorial to Christopher who said to me more than once. "Mama do you think I will ever be famous? That is what I want is to be famous."

Jacob's place is now open and many children are enjoying a safe relaxing place to play and learn how to interact with others. One night a week Jake and his Mom tutor these children. Any weekend you might find Jake teaching them how to play chess. Jake's Dad and Mom plan games that are easy for each to participate. One week it might be teaching them golf using soft material equipment and the next week baseball with the same type of soft material. The idea is to present an atmosphere of fun and accomplishment in a safe environment where no one will criticize or make fun but instead cheer them on to victory. For some children just tossing a soft ball a few feet is a big deal for them. These sessions are directed by Jakes Mom and Dan and aided by the parents of the children. After this time of directed play they are free to play on their own and most of them choose to shoot baskets. There is a basketball show case with Christopher's name and displayed in it is one of Christopher's basketballs.

$$\text{The Accident}$$

This was an accident waiting to happen. That is exactly what it was, an accident that should never have happened. No one set out to deliberately kill Christopher. It was a combination of several misguided decisions that all came together at a point in time that caused the loss of my ten year old. The path he had to maneuver to get to the sidewalk was treacherous and no one was watching or waiting for him that day to arrive safely. This set the stage for the chain of events to come. Taken all together there was a failure in the responsibility to keep him safe

I drove Christopher to his home school in the morning and picked him up after school at the same place. He got out of my car and right into the bus that took him to his special classes at another school. When I picked him up at his home school a teacher walked him to the car and opened the door and saw that he was safe in my car. I had no reason to even think that the situation would be different at another school in the same school district. He was let off his bus in an area where he had to cross the parking lot through parked cars and across the path of the buses and cars onto the safety of the sidewalk.

Because of this accident the schools in the state of Indiana took another look at their drop off and pick up pattern. Many have changed their system and definitely all are more aware now of the importance of a safe pick up and drop off system for the precious cargo they carry every day.

I know someone who knows the woman who was driving the bus that killed Christopher. She is devastated about the accident. I put myself in her position and thought I too would feel the same and probably would have flash backs of the accident the rest of my life and my heart aches for her. I prayed for all concerned that day and still continue to pray for this woman. She has sad memories of the accident and has even gone to Christopher's grave but the closure she seeks doesn't happen. I harbor no ill will toward her and on the advice of my pastors would gladly meet with her at the church if this would help her. So far this meeting has not taken place.

Since the accident I have met people who prayed for us that day and they had no idea who we were. God has been so gracious to allow us to meet so long after the accident. One lady said she drove by the school and saw all the fire trucks and police and red lights and knew something really bad had happened. She pulled over and sat outside the school for an hour praying. What a blessing to finally meet her.

My house is for sale and a family came to view the house and when they saw the pictures on the wall of Christopher and Hannah they asked about them. When I told them they said, "We prayed for you when we heard, not knowing you but that doesn't matter in a case like this."

Both of the children liked to go with me grocery shopping at a small store near our house. We became acquainted with one of the cashier's and she and the children talked about what was happening in their lives that particular day but names were never mentioned. When I finally was able to go shopping again I told her that was Christopher in the school bus accident. Without saying a word she went immediately to the flower section and retrieved the largest bouquet of roses and thrust them into my arms and with tears in her eyes gave me a hug. Those roses lasted for two weeks but the gesture of shared sorrow remains today.

The children and I very often visited the Dairy Queen and the woman who waited on us was so taken with the two of them. Christopher would engage her in some of the longest conversations, asking her questions about how the ice cream is made and any other topic of his interest on that particular day. She was delighted when they came into the store to talk with her. When it was his birthday she would decorate his cake and free hand draw the, what else, guitar. One year she even made a trip to the grocery to get some added decorations for his cake. I went to see her a couple weeks after the accident and she came out from behind the counter and hugged me and cried with me and told me again how much she looked forward to Christopher's conversation's her.

Several months after the accident I received a large thick packet from my lawyer. I assumed it was more information about the legal side of the accident. There was no cover letter to let me know what it contained so I proceeded to open it and flip through the pages. It took me seeing a word here and a word there before I realized what I was reading. I screamed and threw the pages across the room. I had been so careful not to read the newspaper or watch the news about the accident. I was so afraid I would hear details that I couldn't handle and now I had in my hand the coroner's accident report and I nearly lost it over this insensitive mailing sent to me without warning as to what it contained. When your heart is ripped open from a tragedy any little thing such as this report can rip your heart afresh. I began to think I would never get through this hurtful tender time and all I wanted to do was to pull the covers over my head and cry or sleep or die. These are the times you must keep your faith and cling to Jesus. Some people have to deal with questioning their faith when hit with a tragedy but that was never my problem. If you do struggle with questioning your faith encouragement will be there for you as you stay in the Word, and continue to pray, even when you don't feel like it, even when you think the words will stick in your throat. Keep in contact with friends who will bring comfort to you as they encourage you to get out of bed, get back into life again even though you feel it is the last thing you want to do. I also believe that it is not wrong to give in to these things for a while until healing can begin to take hold. There is no time limit and everyone handles sorrow differently but this I know; The LORD is near the brokenhearted and saves those who are crushed in spirit." Psalm 34:18

~10~

Adopted Into the Family

*L*est you think Christopher was a little angelic child with a visible halo on his head let me assure you he was not. He was a typical little boy who got into plenty of situations. He had a temper at times and could be aggressive especially with his little sister. But then she could push his buttons also. If any of you reading this have more than one child you know what I am saying. To this day I cannot explain some of the things Christopher did and he couldn't either. He constantly took things apart but never back together. I finally learned if I was missing something from the house or garage it could usually be found in the woods or over the fence in the woods. It could be the good silver or the electric leaf blower or Hannah's stuffed animal. One never knew what it would be. My daily laundry was enough for a house full of kids. It wasn't that he changed clothes several time but that he layered clothes on himself all day. By the end of the day he might peel from his body four different outfits. He would put jelly on the bread before putting it in the toaster. He went through three toasters! I taught him how to cook breakfast and on Saturday's that was his job and what a good job he did. Forget the clean up! He loved to eat and would give me a bear hug and tell me I was a good cook. Aside from his occasional outburst he was the most loving child I have ever known and he loved to be loved and hugged. Sometimes children with problems like Jake's and Christopher's don't like to be touched but that was not so with Christopher.

About a year before the accident Christopher began having various problems. He couldn't stand to touch paper; it would give his skin a sensation that would disturb him. He had headaches and his behavior toward Hannah was aggressive. For about two years Hannah had spent every weekend with my son and his wife which helped to give me a little break. Because of this the decision for her to live with them permanently was not a difficult one. Christopher needed much attention and Hannah needed to be safe. The decision was easy but the carrying out of it was hard on me. I had raised her from five months and she was now six years. I was her Mommy. My son and his wife and I talked to her and she seemed to understand it would be safer for her to stay with them. With this set up I could work with Christopher one on one. She did have some adjustment but for the most part she adjusted very well to her new surroundings. We were all still together on holidays and birthdays and many other times. I spent the next several months having every kind of test I could think have done on Christopher to see if there was anything that triggered this change. The entire set of tests was negative. He was a very healthy child. His behavior improved and I tried to keep him from situations that would be hard for him to handle.

A year after the accident Hannah was adopted by my son and his wife. Our family is no stranger to adoption. In fact it is the norm with us and a biblical concept. Scripture tells us we are adopted into God's family. Ephesians 1:5 is about our adoption as sons through Jesus Christ to Himself according to the kind intention of His will. Similar passages are found in Galatians 4:4-7 and Romans 8:15-17. My grandparents had nine birth children and in their sixties they adopted a baby. My husband and I took in our two grandchildren in our sixties. I am adopted by my aunt and uncle and both of my children are adopted.

Hannah is now part of a family with three college age siblings and they love and accept her as their sister. Hannah struggles with Christopher's death and especially when she spends time with me in my home. It seems as if the memories stay with her and she doesn't know how to handle her emotions once her visit is over and she returns to her new home.

Hannah had her tenth birthday in January which was just a few weeks before the third anniversary of the accident. Hannah declared now that she was the age Christopher was when he died she too wanted to die. That came out of the blue for all of us and we are working with her to alleviate those fears.

She still wonders why the ambulance did not come and take Christopher to the hospital where he would get well. Some things are difficult to explain and even more difficult for her to understand completely. Hannah is doing very well in her school work and this makes us so thankful that she is free of any of the academic problems Christopher had. However I am sorry to say there have been incidences at school that have devastated her. She has been teased by other students about the death of Christopher. These situations have been dealt with very well by the faculty but does not erase the memory of this cruel teasing.

Christopher also was on the receiving end of children's taunting words. One day he came in from playing and said "Mama what does retard mean?" I knew exactly what had happened and it made me sad for him and I assured him he did not fit the meaning of the word and it was not a word that should be used. I gave him a big hug and it seemed to satisfy him. Children need to be assured their identity comes from being a child of God not from any names they are called and they are special in Gods eyes.

My daughter has been crushed by the loss of Christopher. She really loved Christopher but could not take care of him. Since she doesn't drive I would pick her up and bring her to the house so she could visit with the children. She is like another playmate to them. She had Petit Mal seizures as a young child which made school work difficult for her. The teacher needed to sit beside her to give her an assignment because she had a hand to eye coordination problem where she could not transfer letters from the blackboard to her paper. We had her extensively tested in every area to find what we could do for her but there was never much offered to us. I believe now there would be help for her that was not available when she was a child. Something very good has come from this for my daughter and me. This has changed her prayer life and brought her to much reflection about her life and choices I told her if she wants to see Christopher again she needs to be sure she is saved and going to heaven. Our relationship has changed and softened. It seems to have taken the fight out of her. She talks now about her prayers and her belief. We still have many crying sessions together. She is in complete agreement with Hannah's adoption and wants only the best for her and they still see each other often.

11

Heartache for Jake

Jake has had a very difficult time with the death of Christopher. When his mom told him of Christopher's death she said he curled up on the couch and let out a scream that she hopes she never has to hear ever again from a person. He cried and screamed like this for three days. She said to this day he is still not the same. He surrounded himself in his room with Christopher's toys and pictures and slept with the toys. His Mom said he finally cried himself out. She said she didn't know anyone could cry so many tears. He wants to talk to me and be with me because this makes him feel close to Christopher. He said he wanted to be Christopher. The Barnett family and I went out to eat after church one Sunday shortly after the accident and Jake wanted to ride in my car with me. He wanted to sit in Christopher's seat. He needed to feel close to something that reminded him of Christopher. When we got to the restaurant he asked me "Now, what would Christopher have ordered?" I told him and that is what he ordered and ate.

The first anniversary of the accident was another day of Jake crying all day for Christopher. The second year was a repeat of the first. The third year seemed to be even worse than the others. The anniversary date was on a Monday which was the next day after the Super Bowl. Jake attends a University in the downtown area where the Super Bowl was held. That whole area was so inundated with Super Bowl atmosphere even on the day after. Jake cried so hard his Professor had to take him to another room and let him cry. Super Bowl Sunday was the last time Jake had talked to Christopher. They spent the entire game time on the phone working on magic tricks that Christopher was going to show to his class mates on the next Friday. Jake was eager to get home that day to call Christopher and talk about the magic tricks but instead he was told of his death.

Jake's high IQ and his visit to New York City to be on Glen Beck's program and Sixty Minutes program have brought him much attention. He has received calls from people in all walks of life from around the world. His mother ask him how he felt about all this attention he was getting. Without hesitating his answer was "My friend Christopher always wanted to be famous." It is my opinion one of the reasons the two of them had so much fun and the fact Jake misses him so much was due to the fact Christopher loved to play. Jakes brain never shuts down from all the information in his mind. His mother told me a long time ago she would see his light on in the late night hours and when she checked he would be writing formulas. I believe when he was with Christopher he could be just another kid playing and having fun. I think he longs for those times again. It was a good time in his childhood that will never be again. My hope is he will remember these times all his life but not with such deep sadness but with joy and hope of seeing Christopher again, his childhood friend

Conclusion

Reflections

Losing Christopher from my life here on earth has been the most traumatic event so far in my life. I have had other situations in my life that have been hard to handle and have disrupted my life but I have always had something to work with to eventually set things right. With this there was nowhere to go. Christopher was dead; end of story. When my husband died we were not surprised. We knew about how long he had to live when we found the treatment was no longer working. The aggressive Lymphoma had not manifested itself at the onset of the disease, but now it had and we had time to deal with the inevitable

With Christopher there was no warning. One minute he was alive and literally the next minute he was dead. It's a wonder I didn't die during those first months and I wished I would. I had such a deep agonizing hurt that would not go away. The shock to my physical body has taken a toll on my strength and has instilled in me a sadness hidden from others but lingers deep in my being where only God can see and reach. This is how it should be, safe with my Lord who never stops comforting and encouraging me and understanding my aching heart.

Some people get mad at God when such a tragedy happens but that was never in my thoughts. Never would I blame God for any of this. I didn't want to be like Job's wife in Job 2:9-10. Job went through a rough time when he lost everything. A messenger came to give him bad news and before the words were out of the messenger's mouth another was there to give him more bad news. Job's wife said to him, "Do you still hold fast your integrity? Curse God and die!" Job's answer was "Shall we indeed accept good from God and not accept adversity?" In all this Job did not sin with his lips".

I can't say I understand fully why this had to happen in the way it did but I know the Sovereignty of God covers life and death. I cried out Psalm 119:16 over and over again to reassure myself from the Word that God was and is in charge of Christopher's life."You have seen Christopher's unformed substance; and in Thy book they were all written, the days that were ordained for Christopher, when as yet there was not one of them."

I refuse to have the joy of the Lord taken from me by the enemy. I will keep my dark times for just the Lord and me and not burden others with a sad countenance or a useless life. I am a survivor and Jesus tells me so, "I am more than a conqueror in Jesus Christ." Romans 8:37. "I can do all things through Christ Who strengthens me." Philippians 4:13. In other words He infuses me with His strength for I have none of my own. For a very long time after the accident when I would go to bed I could not sleep because I could not get the events of the accident out of my mind and when I did drift off I would awaken to be faced with more hours of deep desperation for peace. I cried out to the

Lord so many times that I needed to have His peace. I quoted every Scripture I had learned concerning His sovereignty, and His peace. I searched my mind for what I had learned about His names and what they meant. In the night watches I repeated out loud to the Lord what I had learned from my Bible studies. I wondered if I would ever stop crying and I certainly played out Psalm 6:6 "I am weary with my sighing, every night I make my bed swim, I dissolve my couch with my tears." Slowly, little by little as I rested in what I knew to be truth I finally got to the point of peaceful rest. When I reflected on the crucifixion and really dwelt on Jesus sacrifice that He willingly made on Calvary's cross I had nowhere to go with self-pity. That is when I would collapse into His arms. Jesus said to the twelve disciples, "You do not want to go away also, do you?" Peter's response was, "Lord to whom shall we go? You have words of eternal life." John 6:68. I'm with Peter; I am not going anywhere but with Jesus!

What about you, do you know Jesus Christ as your Lord and Savior? This is the beginning of your journey from dark into light. John 18:12 says "I am the light of the world; he Who follows Me shall not walk in the darkness, but shall have the light of life." And again Acts 4:12 "And there is salvation in no one else for there is no other name under heaven that has been given among men, by which we must be saved."

I would offer to anyone going through the loss of a loved one to give yourself over to the Lord. Understand for your peace of mind and acceptance of your tragedy you need to release the grief in you to the Lord. This may not come easy at first and with each person the time it takes will be different. I urge you to keep going to the Scripture and reading it over and over out loud to Him. Read it with the assurance it is truth and God loves you so much. He will be there through every tear you shed. He is the great Comforter. Eventually that truth, that assurance, that peace will seep deep into your heart imbedded forever. Dwell on this awesome power and His goodness. Philippians 4:6, 7 tells us "Be anxious for nothing, but in everything by prayer and supplication with thanksgiving let your requests be made known to God And the peace of God which surpasses all comprehension, shall guard your hears and your minds in Christ Jesus." In other words God's peace that He gives surpasses our understanding. It goes beyond what we are able to comprehend. This is what I was striving for in my dark journey through grief and He didn't disappoint.

Scripture tells us to cast our burdens upon the Lord because He cares for us. Even with this knowledge I have those times when something triggers a memory and I have this deep pain inside of me that is as fresh as the moment I heard of the accident and here come the tears again. At times like this it's O.K. to let your tears flow no matter how many or how long. I think of the tears Jake has shed for Christopher and it reminds me God has a bottle for our tears. Psalm 56:8b "Put my tears in Thy bottle; Are they not in Thy book?" What I am finding is when I pray about this deep hurt, my prayers turn to a cry to the Lord for the children. "Lord protect the children, those being abused, neglected, those with terminal illnesses and especially those with conditions such as autism and the entire spectrum of this type of condition." I pray for the parents who are bone weary from the constant responsibility to protect these children, sometimes from themselves, often from other children who are not always kind to a child who is different, to adults who are unaware of these needs, especially if their children are healthy. There are so many children who are never taken to church or never told about Jesus and my heart aches for them.

I do believe that heaven is a real place and has a special place for these little ones. The word heaven is mentioned in Scripture at least four hundred and fifty seven times. As recorded in John 14:1-3 at the last supper Jesus gives a promise to His disciples about heaven. "Let not your heart be troubled; believe in God, believe also in Me. In my Father's house are many dwelling places; if it were not so, I would have told you; for I go to prepare a place for you. And if I go and prepare a place for you, I will come again, and receive you to Myself; that where I am, there you may be also." In Matthew 18: 1-6, 10 Jesus is talking to His disciples about children and heaven. "At that time the disciples came to Jesus, saying, Who then is greatest in the kingdom of heaven?" And He called a child to Himself and set him before them, and said, "Truly I say to you, unless you are converted and become like children, you shall not enter the kingdom of heaven. "Whoever then humbles himself as this child, he is the greatest in the kingdom of heaven." "See that you do not despise one of these little ones, for I say to you, that their angels in heaven continually behold the face of My Father who is in heaven." It seems as if God has appointed special angels to care for the children in heaven. Christopher may well indeed be playing with angels.

In the fall before the accident Christopher planted a flower seed in a neighbor's yard. In the spring of the next year my neighbor presented me with the most vibrantly colored blossom I had ever seen and only then did I know he had planted the seed. When a flower seed is planted there is hope that in its season it will burst forth in all its beauty as it was meant to be. This is a visual picture of Jesus words about heaven. By faith I believe Christopher has "burst forth", has blossomed into all he was created to be.

I picture Christopher in heaven where he knows he is taken care of and safe. He used to worry about what would happen to him when I die. "Mama what will happen to me, who will take care of me when you die and you are going to die soon because you are getting old!" Don't you love the honesty and bluntness of kids? I can see his engaging smile, his bright eyes and wonderment at all that he is seeing and doing in heaven.

I picture the time I join him and he says "Mama, come look at this, isn't it wonderful, oh look at this, and oh come look at this, remember you told me about this." He was always so excited about heaven while here on earth that I can imagine that excitement intensified for all eternity. Yes, Christopher is exactly where he was born to be...heaven He has come full circle according to Philippians 3:20. "For our citizenship is in heaven, from which also we eagerly wait for a Savior, the Lord Jesus Christ;"

I am so grateful to my church for their continued support and their desire to teach Jesus and His Word to the children and their parents. Several times the Pastor will teach a series on a certain subject or book in the Bible and the children's program will be coordinated with the same teaching each week so during the week there can be a family discussion of the lesson. One of these times as we were leaving church I ask Christopher what he learned and as he told me I said "We learned the same thing today." He stopped walking and looked at me and said with a big grin and that excited look he would get when he talked about Jesus and said "You mean they talk about God in the big room too? WOW." This is what makes precious memories!

Parents, grandparents, teachers fill the minds and hearts of these little ones with Jesus before the world system gets imbedded in them. You may think they are too young to understand but they will remember a word here and a word there and others will build on the foundation you have laid.

They may be in the autistic spectrum but they can still learn about Jesus. Give them something that is eternal; instill in them a love of church and Jesus at an early age. Protect them from all the destroying elements in the world they will encounter as they grow by talking about Jesus just as if He were there in the flesh.

Grief

What is grief and how do you describe or explain it to someone? The dictionary says it is a deep sorrow or mental distress and the extreme of grief is anguish, which tortures or terrifies the spirit. Everyone handles grief in their own way and if ask each would have a different description of how grief manifest itself in their situation. However you describe your grief the goal is to get beyond it, to not let it overwhelm you to the point you no longer are able to function in life. This is a process and how long it takes will be different for each person. If you are going through grief give yourself time to heal, don't feel guilty thinking you are taking too long. If you are a friend of one grieving be patient with them, pray with and for them. One of the comforting things for me was I had friends who would let me talk about Christopher and even more important they talked about him. Just hearing his name was special to me. I want Christopher's memory to be kept alive especially for Hannah but not in a morbid way but in a joyous, gentle reflecting manner.

It has been difficult to relive those first minutes and hours and days after the accident. I finally have been able to at least in part express the deep hurt of the initial shock. I still am not sure I have captured completely the depth of the agony of losing a child. When Christopher was taken from this world so unexpected and quickly I was ripped apart deep in my soul. My grief was on a level I had never experienced before. Both my parents and my husband and several dear friends have died and I grieved for them and still miss them. However this grief of losing a child was different. It was a new kind of grief and it tore my soul apart with such agony that I knew I would never recover. It was so scary I thought I would die and I even prayed I would.

When I was given the news so abruptly it affected my body. I could feel it in my body and I hurt but it wasn't a physical pain. It was as if my body had been ripped open and my life's blood was pouring out of me yet there was no physical pain. This kind of agony goes much deeper. There were no words of comfort that reached me where I was in this unknown scary place I now found myself. My grief was smothering the life from me. I was very much like a person in need of trauma room measures. I had a severe gaping wound in my soul and I needed tender care, medicine, rest and encouragement from my Healer Jesus. He did not let me down. He never left my side during the critical hours and His medicine was His Word and the encouragement was the friends He sent. God comforts us Himself but His comfort also comes through people who minister to us.

2 Corinthians 1:3, 4 tells us that he is the God of all comfort who comforts us in all our affliction so that we will be able to comfort others. Did you catch the last part of that statement, that we are comforted so we might comfort others? This is one of my reasons for writing this book. If you have gone through

the trauma of losing a child I want my story to encourage and comfort you. I pray you gain strength from God's Word that has been included in this writing. What better way to comfort others than to give them the Word of God. The letters and cards and encouragement I received with Scripture written on them were my comfort and strength. Psalm 119:50 says "This is my comfort in my affliction that your word has revived me." I feel blessed that I had so much of God's Word already stored in my heart. I didn't have the struggle of trying to know God at this hurtful time. I knew Him and I knew His promises and His love and that is where my healing and strength came. If you are not in an in depth Bible study I urge you to run not walk to the nearest one. How much easier to go through difficulties if you know the Lord and have His Word hidden in your heart.

Has your world come apart? Are you in a dark place in your life and it seems as if you will never get back into the light again. Are you asking, will life ever be the same again? Will I ever laugh again? Yes, yes you will. It will get better. You will be a survivor. Jesus wants you to survive and thrive in this world. He is our High Priest and He makes intercession for us. When you are in the midst of your sorrow and cannot pray, He is praying for you. You are never alone. No one is immune to the sorrows and trials of the world but this I know Jesus is with you in any deep dark valley of grief that you encounter. In fact he has already been there before you and has prepared for you beautiful treasures as He walks that path with you. It has been said that explorers have found places that no one has ever been before and there they have found the most unusual beautiful flowers blooming they have ever seen.

This is so like God to go before us to prepare the way he knows we will have to travel. Flowers remind me of life, hope and beauty and in the deepest darkest valleys of your life you can be assured that God has gone before and there will be flowers of uncanny beauty along the way. There will be treasures not found on the broad path of life but in the deepest narrowest valleys. Losing a child certainly puts you in a deep valley. Jesus says I will never leave you or forsake you. He is with you no matter and as strange as it sounds He has many blessings in store for you as you go through the sorrow of losing your beloved child or another loved one. As you go through the dark valley of despair you may have to step on thorns that hurt but Jesus has gone before and taken the poison out of the thorns so you are not drained completely of your life.

You will come to know God in a way you never have before. There will be quite intimate times when it is just you and the Lord as He, through His Word, begins the healing process. There were times when I was in such despair over the accident yet I knew God was with me in this darkness for in my spirit I could almost feel the breath of God upon me. I felt a sense of wellbeing when I was at my lowest because He promised He would not leave me. I will never "get over" what happened to Christopher but I am getting through it. Jesus has brought me safely through the dark journey of grief into His marvelous light and healing. The rawness of the wound is healing but the scar will always be there. There will always be a hurt in my soul and I will have flashbacks forever of the accident but I am getting better about handling them when they hit my mind. My mind is seldom free from thinking of Christopher and that I do not want to lose but I want the memories to bring a smile instead of deep pain.

My encouragement to you is that you will get through this and will be stronger in your faith and have beautiful stories and memories to cherish in your heart until you are united with your child or loved one again.

"I would have despaired unless I had believed I would see the goodness of the Lord in the land of the living. Wait for the Lord; Be strong and let your heart take courage." Psalm 27:13-14

Christopher and Jake

Resources

FREEWHEELIN.ORG

Precept Ministries International
www.precept.org
800.763.8280
Precept Ministries International
P.O. Box 182218
Chattanooga, TN 37422

myjacobsplace@gmail.com

T hree deaths of family members in four years, including my husband, did not prepare me for the words I was hearing from the police chief. "Christopher has been killed by a school bus." Death did not come quietly that cold February morning but crashed into my life like a destroying tornado. The tragic death of my ten-year-old grandson, whom I was raising, set me on a deep, dark journey into grief. This was a frightening journey I had never traveled before, and I didn't want to be on this path of despair. I was not alone, for a gracious, loving, sovereign God journeyed with me through this strange, unknown valley and brought me through to victory. Someday there will be a final victory over death, as we see in Scripture.

Revelation 21:4: *"And He shall wipe away every tear from their eyes; and there shall no longer be any death; there shall no longer be any mourning, or crying, or pain the first things have passed away."*

Phyllis Betz, a lifelong resident of Indianapolis, Indiana, is a widowed mother of two grown children and grandmother of five. She is a former Precept Workshop trainer and currently leads a Precept Inductive Bible Study class in Indianapolis. This is her first book, but she has written articles for her church blog and inspirational messages for women's conferences in Indianapolis.

InspiringVoices®
A Service of **Guideposts**